China's
Hidden Narratives

Exploring Forbidden Discussions

Tommy C. Owen

Copyright © Tommy C. Owen, 2024.

All rights reserved. No part of this publication may be reproduced, distributed, or transmitted in any form or by any means, including photocopying, recording, or other electronic or mechanical methods, without the prior written permission of the publisher, except in the case of brief quotations embodied in critical reviews and certain other noncommercial uses permitted by copyright law.

CONTENTS

Prologue

Unveiling the Hidden Threads of a Complex Society

    The Allure of China: A Global Powerhouse

    Understanding 'Forbidden Discussions'

Part I: Historical Shadows

    The Legacy of the Cultural Revolution

    The Tiananmen Square Incident: A Silenced Tragedy

    Ethnic Minorities: Voices from the Margins

Part II: Economic Growth and Social Consequences

    The Cost of Modernization

    The Rise of the '996' Work Culture

    Invisible Inequalities

Part III: The Cultural Perspective

    Art and Literature Under Surveillance

    The Role of Social Media

    Gender and LGBTQ+ Issues

Part IV: The Political Landscape

    The Changing Role of Media

    China's Foreign Policy and Hidden Agendas

    The Future of Free Speech in China

Conclusion

    A Call to Awareness and Empathy

Prologue

In a world where information flows freely for some and is tightly controlled for others, the right to speak and be heard remains a battleground. Across history, voices have been silenced—by oppressive governments, corporate interests, and even the invisible forces of social pressure. Yet, even in the darkest moments of suppression, truth finds a way to surface.

The fight for free speech is not just about law or politics; it is about humanity's fundamental need to share ideas, challenge norms, and seek justice. When voices are stifled, stories go untold, and perspectives are lost, weakening the collective understanding of our world. But what if those who are free to speak chose to amplify the voices of those who are not? What if global citizens took it upon themselves to uncover hidden truths, refusing to let silence be the final word?

Nowhere is this struggle more evident than in China, where tightly controlled narratives shape both domestic and international perceptions. The Chinese people live under a sophisticated system of censorship that dictates what can be known, what can be questioned, and what must remain hidden. Yet beneath the official narratives, countless stories of resilience, courage, and quiet defiance exist. Understanding these hidden truths does not merely reveal the reality of life under state control—it fosters empathy, connecting people across borders through shared struggles for freedom.

This book is a call to action. It is an exploration of the power of speech, the consequences of its suppression, and the ways in which individuals can resist silence. In reading these pages, you step into a world where words have power, where truth is a form of resistance, and were amplifying the silenced can shape the course of history.

Unveiling the Hidden Threads of a Complex Society

China is a country that captures the imagination of the world. With its rich history, economic power, and complex social fabric, it stands as both a global powerhouse and a cultural enigma. But beyond the headlines and tourist brochures lies a reservoir of untold stories that are essential to understanding the full spectrum of China's identity. Let's unpack why the world is so captivated by this nation and why delving into its hidden narratives is more crucial than ever.

The Allure of China: A Global Powerhouse

1. **Economic Might on the World Stage**
   China's meteoric rise from a developing nation to the world's second-largest economy is nothing short of extraordinary. Its role as the "factory of the world" has transformed global supply chains and introduced affordable products to millions. Yet, the price of this economic success—environmental degradation, worker exploitation, and rapid urbanization—remains a largely untold story.
2. **A Civilization Steeped in History**
   Few nations can boast a continuous civilization spanning over 5,000 years. From the Great Wall to the Silk Road, China's historical contributions to art, science, and trade

have left an indelible mark on humanity. But how much of that history is openly discussed within its borders? Events like the Cultural Revolution and the opium wars are pivotal yet shrouded in curated narratives.

3. **Cultural Soft Power**
The global spread of Chinese cuisine, martial arts, and cinema highlights the country's cultural influence. Meanwhile, its unique blend of Confucian traditions and modern innovations draws curiosity. Beneath this cultural celebration, however, lies a tension between preservation and state intervention, a story often hidden from global view.

Why the World Is Fascinated by China

1. **The Duality of Tradition and Modernity**
China presents an intriguing paradox: a nation rooted in centuries-old traditions yet surging ahead in cutting-edge technology. Cities like Shanghai and Shenzhen are showcases of futuristic architecture and innovation, but nearby villages may still rely on practices that have endured for generations. This duality makes China both relatable and mysterious.

2. **Geopolitical Influence**
As a permanent member of the United Nations Security Council and a major player in global trade, China's actions ripple across the world. Its Belt and Road Initiative, for instance, connects dozens of countries through infrastructure projects, reshaping geopolitics. These grand strategies often overshadow the voices of local communities affected by such projects.

3. **A Complex Political Landscape**
China's unique political system, marked by single-party rule, attracts both admiration and criticism. Its

rapid economic development is often contrasted with strict control over free speech and dissent. The balancing act between governance, progress, and individual freedoms is a story that deserves closer examination.

The Importance of Exploring Untold Stories

1. **Understanding the Human Cost of Progress**
   Behind the skyscrapers and mega-projects are individuals whose lives are profoundly impacted by China's transformation. Farmers displaced by urbanization, factory workers enduring grueling hours, and citizens navigating censorship are stories that need to be heard to understand the real cost of modernization.
2. **Challenging One-Dimensional Narratives**
   Much of the world views China through a limited lens—either as a threat to global stability or as an economic miracle. Exploring untold stories helps break down these simplistic narratives, revealing a more nuanced and humanized portrait of the nation.
3. **Fostering Global Empathy**
   In an increasingly interconnected world, understanding the struggles, dreams, and resilience of ordinary Chinese citizens can bridge cultural divides. It reminds us that despite differing systems and histories, we share universal values of dignity, freedom, and hope.

Hidden narratives offer a lens into the intricate layers of Chinese society, unveiling truths that official accounts often obscure. These stories, frequently suppressed or overlooked, provide a richer and more authentic understanding of the challenges, complexities, and contradictions that define modern China. By uncovering these silenced voices, one can gain insight into the lived realities of ordinary people, the tension between tradition and modernity, and the impact of rapid development on individuals and communities.

Chinese society is shaped by its history, culture, and governance, yet the state-driven narrative often simplifies or sanitizes this complexity. Hidden narratives, such as personal accounts from the Cultural Revolution or reflections on the Tiananmen Square protests, challenge this homogeneity by revealing how individuals experienced these events. These perspectives add depth to the historical record, showing how policies and political movements affected people on a deeply personal level.

In addition to historical insights, hidden narratives expose the undercurrents of contemporary life in China. For example, stories from workers in factories navigating the pressures of the '996' work culture—working from 9 a.m. to 9 p.m., six days a week—highlight the human cost of economic growth. Similarly, the experiences of ethnic minorities such as the Uyghurs or Tibetans illustrate the complexities of identity and cultural preservation in a rapidly modernizing and homogenizing state.

Moreover, these narratives often reveal a delicate balancing act between resistance and conformity. Through art, literature, and digital spaces, many individuals find ways to express dissent or voice concerns despite the constraints of censorship. These creative outlets not only illuminate the resilience of the human spirit but also offer a window into the evolving dynamics of freedom and control within Chinese society.

Ultimately, hidden narratives enrich our understanding by providing a fuller picture of China's social fabric. They remind us that beneath the surface of a seemingly unified nation lies a tapestry of diverse experiences, struggles, and aspirations that shape the collective identity. By engaging with these untold stories, we can better appreciate the complexities of a society that is as multifaceted as it is fascinating.

Understanding 'Forbidden Discussions'

Taboo topics in Chinese culture are shaped by a blend of historical, cultural, and political factors. These topics often fall into categories that challenge social harmony, defy traditional values, or contradict state narratives. Discussing them openly can lead to discomfort, ostracism, or even legal consequences, as the cultural emphasis on harmony and authority makes such conversations sensitive.

One prominent taboo is the discussion of political dissent or critique of the government. Events like the Tiananmen Square protests of 1989 remain tightly controlled subjects, with references censored in media and online platforms. The government's desire to maintain stability and project an image of progress often results in the suppression of stories that challenge this narrative.

Ethnic and religious issues are also sensitive. Topics surrounding the Uyghurs in Xinjiang, the Dalai Lama and Tibet, or the Falun Gong spiritual movement are heavily censored due to their potential to spark dissent or question the state's handling of cultural diversity. Similarly, open discussions about Taiwan's political status or Hong Kong's autonomy are discouraged, as they directly challenge the "One China" policy.

Social taboos include mental health struggles, LGBTQ+ identities, and gender equality issues. While urban centers have seen gradual progress, these subjects remain delicate, particularly in more traditional or rural communities. Family honor and societal expectations often discourage individuals from discussing personal struggles that might bring shame.

Economic disparities, particularly the rural-urban divide, are also uncomfortable topics. While the narrative of China as an economic powerhouse dominates globally, the lived realities of poverty, labor exploitation, and inequality are rarely discussed openly. Highlighting these issues conflicts with the state's image of universal prosperity.

How Do Tradition, Modernity, and Government Policies Influence

Tradition, modernity, and government policies intersect to define the boundaries of acceptable discourse in China. Traditional values, rooted in Confucianism, emphasize respect for authority, family, and social harmony. These principles discourage public debate on contentious issues, as they are seen as threats to collective stability. For example, challenging family decisions, speaking out against elders, or addressing taboo social issues like premarital relationships can conflict with these long-standing values.

Modernity adds another layer of complexity. China's rapid economic development has brought significant social changes, including increased access to education and technology. These shifts have exposed people to diverse ideas, creating tension between traditional norms and modern influences. While younger generations may be more open to discussing topics like mental health or gender identity, societal and familial pressures often keep such conversations constrained.

Government policies, however, play the most decisive role in shaping what can be discussed publicly. The Chinese Communist Party maintains strict control over information through censorship, surveillance, and propaganda. Policies like the Great Firewall limit access to foreign media and platforms, curating what the population can see and discuss online. Sensitive anniversaries, such as June 4th for Tiananmen Square, see heightened scrutiny and the erasure of references, underscoring the government's priority of maintaining a singular narrative.

The state also uses propaganda to promote themes of unity, prosperity, and progress. Topics that contradict or complicate these themes—like environmental degradation, labor rights abuses, or corruption—are suppressed to avoid undermining public confidence. Activists, journalists, and citizens who cross these boundaries face harsh penalties, from social shaming to imprisonment, reinforcing the risks of addressing taboos.

Part I: Historical Shadows

The Legacy of the Cultural Revolution

The Cultural Revolution (1966-1976) was a decade-long political and social upheaval initiated by Mao Zedong, the leader of the Chinese Communist Party (CCP). It aimed to reassert Mao's authority, purge capitalist and traditional elements, and instill communist ideology across Chinese society. However, the campaign led to widespread chaos, violence, and suffering, leaving a lasting scar on the nation.

Key Events of the Cultural Revolution:

1. **Launch of the Cultural Revolution (1966):** Mao mobilized the Red Guards, a youth-driven movement, to attack the "Four Olds"—old customs, culture, habits, and ideas. Schools and universities were shut down, and students were encouraged to denounce teachers, intellectuals, and even family members suspected of harboring counter-revolutionary thoughts.
2. **Downfall of Political Rivals (1966-1969):** High-ranking officials, including Liu Shaoqi (then President of China) and Deng Xiaoping, were targeted as "capitalist roaders." Liu was dismissed, publicly humiliated, and later died in custody. Deng was sent to rural exile, although he would later return to power.
3. **Escalation of Violence and Red Guard Factions (1967):** Red Guard factions began fighting one another, leading to violent confrontations. Cities descended into anarchy, and local governance collapsed. Mao ultimately called on

the military to restore order, which further militarized the chaos.

4. **The "Up to the Mountains, Down to the Countryside" Campaign (1968-1970):**
Millions of urban youth were sent to rural areas to "learn from the peasants." This disrupted their education and isolated them from their families, leaving a generation scarred by lost opportunities and alienation.

5. **The Fall of Lin Biao (1971):**
Lin Biao, Mao's designated successor, allegedly attempted a coup and died in a mysterious plane crash. His fall marked a turning point in the revolution, as it exposed cracks within the leadership.

6. **End of the Cultural Revolution (1976):**
Mao's death and the arrest of the Gang of Four, a radical faction led by Mao's wife Jiang Qing, officially ended the revolution. The CCP denounced the movement as a "catastrophe" in 1981, attributing it to Mao's errors.

How the Cultural Revolution Is Remembered Today:

Official narratives in China minimize discussion of the Cultural Revolution, framing it as a deviation rather than a defining moment. Public commemoration is rare, and open discourse is discouraged due to its sensitive nature. However, the period remains a symbol of suffering and resilience for those who lived through it.

Outside of China, the Cultural Revolution is widely studied as an example of ideological extremism and its devastating societal consequences. Academics and historians emphasize its role in shaping modern China's political, social, and cultural landscape.

Survivor testimonies provide invaluable insight into the human cost of the Cultural Revolution, exposing the deep scars left on Chinese society. These accounts, often shared through memoirs, interviews, and oral histories, reveal the period's profound emotional, social, and psychological toll.

1. Humanizing the Statistics:
While official records document millions of deaths and countless cases of persecution, personal accounts bring these numbers to life. Survivors recount harrowing experiences of public humiliation, imprisonment, and forced labor. Their stories illustrate how families were torn apart as individuals were coerced into betraying loved ones.

2. The Loss of a Generation's Education:
Many survivors describe the long-term impact of the "Up to the Mountains, Down to the Countryside" campaign. For many urban youth, this period represented years of lost education, shattered aspirations, and grueling rural labor. Their experiences highlight how the revolution disrupted the intellectual and professional potential of an entire generation.

3. Fear and Mistrust in Society:
Survivor accounts frequently mention the atmosphere of fear and mistrust that pervaded daily life. Accusations could come from anyone—neighbors, colleagues, or even family members. This breakdown of trust had lasting repercussions on social cohesion, with many survivors struggling to rebuild relationships and communities after the revolution.

4. Creativity and Resistance:
Despite the repression, some survivors found ways to resist or document their experiences through art, literature, and underground networks. These narratives reveal the resilience

of the human spirit and the quiet acts of defiance that helped individuals endure the chaos.

The Tiananmen Square Incident: A Silenced Tragedy

The Tiananmen Square protests of 1989, which began as a call for greater political reform and transparency, became one of the most pivotal and tragic moments in modern Chinese history. Yet, for decades, the Chinese government has employed an array of methods to erase or control the narrative surrounding this event. This deliberate censorship and suppression of information play a crucial role in shaping how the Chinese public understands their own history, often to the exclusion of alternative viewpoints.

The Chinese government initially portrayed the protests as a "counter-revolutionary riot" and sought to paint the demonstrators as violent, destabilizing forces. In the immediate aftermath of the crackdown, the state-controlled media quickly shut down coverage of the events. This erasure of information extended to textbooks, official histories, and public speeches, where any mention of the protests was minimized or outright omitted. Over the years, the government has maintained a strict policy of censorship, ensuring that the true extent of the violence and the scale of the protests are not accessible to most Chinese citizens.

One of the most significant tools used to control the narrative is the Great Firewall, China's internet censorship system. The government actively monitors and blocks online discussions, removing references to the protests from websites and social media platforms. Keywords related to Tiananmen Square, like "June Fourth" or "Tank Man," are heavily filtered, making it nearly impossible for ordinary citizens to search for accurate information on the event. The government has also employed strategies like "memory manipulation," where it continues to promote the idea that the event was a necessary action to restore order, framing the crackdown as a justifiable response to an unruly mob.

In addition to media control, the government has made efforts to erase physical reminders of the event. For instance, memorials and exhibitions about the Tiananmen Square protests are banned or heavily restricted. This includes efforts to block overseas Chinese communities from holding commemorative activities, with state-backed organizations targeting activists abroad who attempt to draw attention to the event.

Despite these efforts, Tiananmen Square remains an important, albeit invisible, part of China's collective memory. The government's attempts to erase it only reinforce the emotional weight of the event, creating an atmosphere where the truth is constantly suppressed, and individuals who remember the protests risk persecution for speaking out.

While the Chinese government works tirelessly to control the narrative, the stories of those who participated in or were affected by the Tiananmen Square protests continue to seep through the cracks of state censorship. These personal accounts offer a glimpse into the human side of the tragedy and the enduring impact it had on the lives of countless individuals.

One of the most widely known stories is that of the "Tank Man," the anonymous individual who stood in front of a column of tanks on June 5, 1989, in an act of defiance against the military crackdown. The iconic image of this lone protester facing down military tanks, captured by photojournalists, became a symbol of resistance worldwide. However, despite the widespread recognition of the image, little is known about the identity of the man or his fate. Various accounts suggest that he may have been arrested shortly after the confrontation, but the Chinese government's control of information has ensured that his story remains shrouded in mystery.

For many protesters, the Tiananmen Square protests were an act of idealism—students, intellectuals, and ordinary citizens gathered to demand political reforms, more freedoms, and an end to corruption. Some of the protesters, such as Wang Dan, became prominent figures in the movement. Wang, a student leader, was arrested after the crackdown and sentenced to prison. He was later released, but his life was forever marked by his involvement in the protests. His story of resistance and subsequent exile highlights the personal cost of participating in such a transformative yet dangerous event. Wang, like many others, was forced to navigate life in the shadow of a government that continuously worked to erase his identity as a participant in the protests.

Other participants have shared the deep emotional toll the events of June 1989 had on them. Many were forced to flee the country, seeking asylum in places like the United States, Canada, or Europe, where they could safely discuss the events that had shaped their lives. For these individuals, the trauma of the crackdown has often been compounded by years of silence. Some speak of lost friends and family members who were either killed or disappeared during the military crackdown. These stories are often passed on in whispered conversations, shared in private gatherings, or through underground networks that resist state control.

Even years after the event, those affected by the Tiananmen Square protests continue to live with the scars of their experiences. Some survivors have dedicated their lives to advocating for freedom of expression, while others live in fear of retribution if they speak out. The government's suppression of their stories has led many of them to find other ways to keep the memory alive—through art, writing, and activism in the diaspora. These stories, while at times hidden or fragmented, remind the world of the cost of political freedom and the resilience of those who continue to fight for justice.

Ethnic Minorities: Voices from the Margins

Ethnic minorities in China, such as the Uyghurs, Tibetans, and Mongols, face significant challenges in preserving their cultural heritage and identity. These challenges stem from a combination of state policies, social pressures, and rapid modernization, which often prioritize assimilation over the recognition of cultural diversity.

One of the most prominent challenges is the erosion of language. For many ethnic minorities, language is a cornerstone of cultural identity. In regions like Tibet and Xinjiang, the use of native languages such as Tibetan and Uyghur has been systematically replaced by Mandarin Chinese, particularly in schools and public life. The state's emphasis on Mandarin as the national language is seen as a tool for unifying the country, but it also undermines the ability of these groups to pass on their traditions and heritage to future generations. As younger generations increasingly adopt Mandarin, the risk of losing indigenous languages and, by extension, their unique cultural expressions grows.

Another challenge is the suppression of religious practices. For many ethnic minorities, religion is deeply tied to cultural identity. Tibetans, for instance, follow Tibetan Buddhism, and the Uyghurs practice Islam. However, religious practices are heavily monitored and restricted by the Chinese government. Religious gatherings, religious education, and the display of religious symbols are often restricted, with reports of mosques being demolished and Tibetan Buddhist monks being detained. These restrictions stifle the ability of these communities to live out their faith freely, diminishing the richness of their cultural practices.

Additionally, ethnic minorities are often marginalized in broader society. Despite China's claim to be a multi-ethnic nation, the dominant Han Chinese culture tends to overshadow and marginalize minority cultures. This cultural dominance often results in discrimination in employment, education, and social opportunities for ethnic minorities. In rural areas, these groups struggle with poverty and limited access to resources, while urbanization and government policies push for greater integration into Han Chinese-dominated society, eroding their traditional ways of life.

Lastly, the policies surrounding migration and resettlement programs also pose a significant threat. For instance, the migration of Han Chinese into Xinjiang and Tibet disrupts the local demographic balance and places additional pressures on the resources and culture of ethnic minorities. These policies often lead to tensions and a sense of cultural displacement, as native populations feel their traditional territories are being overrun by outsiders.

How Do Government Policies Shape the Lives of Uyghurs, Tibetans, and Others

Government policies in China have a profound and often detrimental impact on the lives of ethnic minorities, particularly the Uyghurs, Tibetans, and Mongols. The central government's approach to ethnic minorities is heavily influenced by its desire for national unity, political control, and economic development. However, this has often come at the expense of minority cultures and identities.

For the Uyghurs, a Muslim ethnic group predominantly located in Xinjiang, government policies have been marked by intense surveillance, restrictions on religious practices, and forced assimilation. The Chinese government has implemented a range of policies aimed at integrating the Uyghurs into mainstream Chinese society, such as mandatory Mandarin language education, limits on religious expression, and the forced relocation of Uyghur people. Reports of re-education camps, where Uyghurs are allegedly subjected to indoctrination and forced labor, have drawn international condemnation. These policies aim to weaken Uyghur identity by undermining their cultural and religious practices, pushing them to conform to the state's vision of a unified, homogenous China.

Similarly, in Tibet, government policies have been focused on suppressing Tibetan Buddhist practices and promoting the assimilation of Tibetans into mainstream Chinese culture. The Chinese government exercises tight control over religious activities in Tibet, monitoring monasteries and restricting the teachings of the Dalai Lama. Tibetans are encouraged to adopt Mandarin and adopt Chinese cultural practices, while the preservation of traditional Tibetan culture and religion is often framed as a threat to national unity. Tibetans who resist these policies or advocate for greater autonomy are often subjected to harassment, imprisonment, or forced displacement.

The Mongols in Inner Mongolia also face similar pressures, particularly related to language and cultural assimilation. The Chinese government has pushed for Mandarin Chinese to be the dominant language in schools, significantly reducing the use of Mongolian in education and public life. This has sparked protests in recent years, as Mongols fear the loss of their language and heritage. In addition, the Mongolian nomadic lifestyle has been disrupted by government policies promoting sedentary living and state-controlled agriculture, pushing many Mongol people away from their traditional livelihoods.

The state's approach to ethnic minorities is deeply intertwined with its broader policies of economic development and territorial control. For instance, resource extraction projects in Xinjiang, Tibet, and Inner Mongolia often lead to the displacement of indigenous populations.

The government justifies these projects by emphasizing national economic growth, but they frequently come at the expense of local communities who find their lands and ways of life altered or destroyed.

Furthermore, the Chinese government's stance on ethnic minorities has been a tool of political control. The state uses its policies to maintain dominance over regions with large ethnic minority populations. In regions like Xinjiang and Tibet, the heavy military presence and the use of surveillance technologies create a climate of fear and suspicion. The government monitors religious practices, social gatherings, and even private conversations, all in the name of maintaining stability and preventing separatism. The lives of Uyghurs, Tibetans, and other ethnic minorities are thus shaped not only by cultural policies but also by constant surveillance and control.

Part II: Economic Growth and Social Consequences

The Cost of Modernization

China's rapid urbanization over the past few decades has been a defining feature of its economic transformation. Millions of people have moved from rural villages to bustling cities in search of better jobs, education, and living standards. While urbanization has undeniably fueled China's rise as a global economic power, it has also brought with it a range of social and environmental consequences that affect both the quality of life and the natural landscape.

Social Consequences: Fragmented Communities and Inequality

One of the most significant social consequences of rapid urbanization is the displacement and fragmentation of communities. The push for economic development has led to the demolition of entire neighborhoods to make way for new infrastructure, commercial centers, and housing projects. For many, this means leaving behind not just their homes, but the social networks and support systems that were an integral part of their lives.

As rural migrants flood into cities, they often face discrimination and marginalization. While they may find employment in factories or construction, they are frequently relegated to low-paying, unstable jobs with little job security or benefits. The hukou system, which ties citizens to specific regions and limits their access to public services such as healthcare and education based on their registered residence, exacerbates this inequality. Migrants living in cities without the proper hukou status often lack access to social benefits, creating a growing divide between urban elites and migrant workers.

The rapid pace of urbanization has also created a generational gap. Younger generations, who often see cities as hubs of opportunity, may disconnect from their rural roots and traditions, further fracturing the social fabric of rural China. Meanwhile, older generations, who have spent their lives in villages, may struggle to adapt to the fast-paced, impersonal life of the city. This shift not only impacts individual identities but also erodes longstanding community bonds that have held rural society together for centuries.

Environmental Consequences: Strain on Natural Resources

The environmental consequences of rapid urbanization are equally profound. As cities expand, they consume vast amounts of land and natural resources. Large-scale construction projects—whether for housing, roads, or industrial parks—destroy ecosystems, displacing wildlife and leading to habitat loss. Deforestation and the conversion of agricultural land into urban spaces have dramatically altered the landscape, diminishing biodiversity and threatening food security.

The massive migration to cities has also placed tremendous pressure on natural resources such as water and energy. Many cities in China are grappling with severe water shortages, and the demand for clean water increases as the urban population grows. At the same time, air and water pollution from industrial production, traffic, and construction continue to be a significant concern in major urban centers. Smog and polluted rivers are a daily reality for millions of people, contributing to health problems such as respiratory diseases and cancers.

In addition to pollution, rapid urbanization often leads to poor waste management and overcrowding. Cities struggle to manage the increasing volume of waste generated by both residents and industries. Landfills are overflowing, and waste treatment facilities are overwhelmed, contributing to environmental degradation. Urban sprawl also means that infrastructure development—such as public transportation, sewage systems, and sanitation—often lags behind population growth, further compounding environmental issues.

Displacement and Erasure of Communities in the Name of Progress

The pursuit of progress and modernity often comes at the expense of communities that are displaced in the name of urban development. In China, this process is known as "demolition and relocation" (拆迁). Entire neighborhoods, particularly in cities like Beijing, Shanghai, and Chongqing, have been razed to make way for high-rise buildings, shopping malls, and new roads. Residents are typically offered compensation, but the amount often falls short of the value of the homes and communities they are forced to leave behind.

For many, this process is not just about losing a home, but losing a sense of identity and history. These neighborhoods may have been built over generations, and the relationships formed there are deeply embedded in the cultural and social fabric of the community. Once the buildings are demolished, the spaces where families once lived are often replaced with commercial centers or luxury housing, erasing the memories of everyday life and the stories of the people who lived there.

In some cases, entire rural villages have been uprooted to make way for large-scale infrastructure projects like high-speed rail lines or industrial zones. People who have lived in the same area for centuries are forced to move to unfamiliar urban environments where they may not have the skills or resources to thrive. The result is a kind of cultural erasure, where the traditional ways of life are lost, and the communities are scattered, often with little chance of rebuilding the social connections that once defined them.

Even when people are offered new homes or relocation packages, the process of resettlement is rarely smooth. Relocated individuals often find themselves living in high-rise apartment complexes far from the city center, in areas with inadequate infrastructure, or without the social safety nets they had in their original communities. These "new towns" may lack the sense of community that existed in the villages, leading to isolation and mental health challenges for those who are displaced.

The Rise of the '996' Work Culture

The '996' work culture refers to a grueling schedule in which employees work from 9 a.m. to 9 p.m., six days a week—essentially, 72 hours of work per week. It is a term commonly associated with the tech industry in China, especially within fast-growing startups, but its reach extends to other sectors as well. The culture is touted as a sign of dedication, productivity, and ambition, with the expectation that employees will push themselves to the limit for the company's success.

This demanding work schedule is a direct reflection of China's broader economic ambitions. As the world's second-largest economy, China is determined to maintain and expand its position on the global stage. The '996' culture aligns with this drive, where rapid innovation, competition, and growth are prioritized over work-life balance. The model draws inspiration from China's early days of economic reform when hard work and sacrifice were seen as necessary for national progress. This intense work ethic is embedded in the ethos of China's "Chinese Dream," a vision promoted by the government to create a prosperous and powerful nation.

In the tech sector, where global competition is fierce, companies push their employees to meet ever-growing demands for innovation. The desire to compete with Western tech giants like Google, Apple, and Facebook fuels the belief that success requires an unrelenting work pace. For workers, the '996' culture is often seen as a rite of passage—a way to prove loyalty and secure upward mobility within a company.

However, this culture also underscores the immense pressure workers face in an economy that values results over well-being.

At its core, the '996' work culture reflects a society that has made rapid strides toward modernization, but at a steep cost to the individual. It is a symbol of China's economic ambition, where productivity is the measure of success, and personal sacrifice is considered a small price to pay for national glory.

What Are the Personal Stories of Workers Navigating This Grueling Schedule

For many workers in the '996' culture, the reality of this grueling schedule is exhausting and overwhelming. Personal stories from individuals navigating this demanding work life reveal the toll it takes on both their physical health and mental well-being.

One worker, Xiao Li, a software developer in a major Chinese tech company, describes his daily routine as a never-ending cycle. He wakes up at 8 a.m., rushes through breakfast, and heads to the office, where he stays until 9 or 10 p.m. Xiao Li often works through lunch and late into the night to meet deadlines. While he understands that this is the price for career advancement, the constant pressure leaves him drained. "By the time I get home, I don't have the energy to do anything but sleep," he shares. "I don't have a social life anymore. I'm just a cog in the machine."

For others, the pressure of the '996' schedule takes a toll on their health. Zhang Wei, who works as a marketing manager at a startup, recounts experiencing severe burnout after months of overwork. "I started getting headaches and insomnia, but I ignored it. I was scared of being labeled lazy or not committed to the company," she says. Eventually, her health deteriorated to the point where she had to take a medical leave. Even then, she felt guilty, as though stepping away from work made her seem weak in the eyes of her colleagues.

For some, the emotional cost is just as high. Many workers face strained relationships with their families. Li Jun, a father of two and an engineer, admits that he hasn't been able to attend his children's school events or spend quality time with his wife due to his long working hours. "I'm working so much that I barely see my family. My children are growing up, and I'm missing it. But I have to keep going because this is the only way I'll provide for them," he says with a heavy heart.

The toll isn't always evident in the immediate moment, but over time, workers often feel a sense of emptiness. "I'm making money, but I feel like I'm losing my life," says Zhang Wei. She admits that her dreams of a fulfilling career have become tainted by the relentless grind, leaving her questioning whether it's all worth it.

However, not all stories are solely marked by dissatisfaction. Some workers, particularly those just starting out in their careers or those seeking upward mobility, view the '996' culture as a means to an end. For example, Li Hua, a recent college graduate working in a startup, explains, "I know it's tough, but this is how you make your mark. Everyone is working this hard, so I have to as well if I want to succeed."

Yet, there is a growing sense of pushback. A wave of workers, particularly in the tech sector, is beginning to challenge the '996' culture, calling for a healthier work-life balance. Protests and petitions have emerged, with workers demanding better treatment and fewer hours. While the culture remains widespread, these movements signal that the younger generation is starting to question whether success should come at the expense of their health and happiness.

Invisible Inequalities

The wealth gap in China is starkly visible between its urban and rural areas, a divide that has deepened with the country's rapid economic growth. In cities like Beijing, Shanghai, and Shenzhen, economic prosperity is palpable: gleaming skyscrapers, advanced infrastructure, and access to high-paying jobs in technology, finance, and other sectors. The urban elite thrive in these bustling environments, enjoying an ever-expanding middle class, luxury goods, and modern amenities. The promise of China's economic miracle often centers around these urban hubs, painting a picture of success, innovation, and global influence.

However, this growth is not evenly distributed. Rural areas, despite benefiting from some development initiatives, remain significantly behind in terms of income, access to education, healthcare, and job opportunities. Agriculture, which still sustains a large portion of the rural population, is often poorly compensated compared to the high-tech industries flourishing in cities. Moreover, many rural areas struggle with inadequate infrastructure, limited access to healthcare, and poor-quality education, which stifles the potential for upward mobility.

The migration from rural to urban areas, a phenomenon accelerated by China's economic boom, has also contributed to the wealth divide. Millions of rural workers move to cities in search of better-paying jobs, but they often face harsh living conditions and discrimination. These migrant workers are usually relegated to low-paying, physically demanding jobs in construction, factories, and service industries. While they contribute significantly to the urban economy, their earnings are far from sufficient to close the wealth gap, and many live in overcrowded, substandard housing on the outskirts of cities.

This migration also leads to a "left-behind" generation in rural areas—children and elderly parents who are left behind as young adults seek work in the cities. These families experience emotional and economic hardship as the younger generation struggles to send remittances while adjusting to the fast-paced, high-cost life of the urban centers.

The Narratives Reveal the Struggles of Those Left Behind in China's Economic Boom?

The narratives of those left behind in China's economic boom provide a stark contrast to the glossy image of China's success. These stories often paint a picture of hardship, isolation, and frustration, as rural communities grapple with the slow pace of development, migration, and the disparity in opportunities.

One of the most poignant narratives comes from the children left behind in rural areas. With parents migrating to urban centers for work, many children are raised by grandparents or other relatives. These children often face emotional neglect and psychological strain as they deal with the absence of their primary caregivers. Additionally, the quality of education in rural areas is often inferior to that in cities, limiting their opportunities for advancement. As a result, many of these children inherit the same economic struggles their parents faced, perpetuating the cycle of poverty.

Similarly, elderly individuals in rural areas bear the weight of the changing landscape. As their children migrate to cities, many are left to live alone, with limited access to healthcare or social services. These elderly populations experience deep loneliness and economic insecurity, as their pensions, if any, are inadequate to meet the rising costs of living. The traditional family structure, which once offered strong intergenerational support, is weakening in the face of economic pressures and migration.

Migrant workers in cities also share narratives of struggle and resilience. While they seek better-paying jobs in urban centers, many face exploitation and discrimination. They often live in poor conditions in makeshift housing, working long hours for low wages in factories, restaurants, or construction sites. Despite their hard work, they remain ineligible for many of the social benefits that urban residents enjoy, such as healthcare, education for their children, and social security. This exclusion from the urban middle class creates a sense of alienation and highlights the structural inequalities that persist in Chinese society.

Moreover, the booming real estate market and rising cost of living in cities exacerbate the divide. Migrants and lower-income urban residents struggle to afford housing in cities where property prices have surged. This leaves them in precarious living situations, often in overcrowded neighborhoods or temporary housing arrangements on the fringes of the city, far removed from the areas of economic opportunity.

These narratives are often silenced in the official discourse that celebrates China's economic growth. However, through grassroots activism, personal accounts, and some independent journalism, these hidden stories begin to emerge, offering a more nuanced understanding of China's economic success. The struggles of the rural poor, migrant workers, and elderly populations reveal the human cost of China's modernization and economic expansion. They highlight the deep disparities that persist beneath the surface of the country's impressive development, reminding us that prosperity in one part of society often comes at the expense of those left behind.

Part III: The Cultural Perspective

Art and Literature Under Surveillance

Censorship in China profoundly impacts the creative expression of artists and writers, restricting their ability to openly explore themes of political dissent, social inequality, or taboo cultural topics. With the Chinese Communist Party (CCP) maintaining strict control over public discourse, many creative individuals find themselves navigating a minefield of red lines that can lead to severe consequences if crossed. These restrictions are not just about preventing overt political commentary, but about controlling the narrative of national identity, societal values, and cultural harmony.

For artists and writers, this often means working within a framework that prioritizes the state's agenda over individual creativity. Literature, visual arts, and even film and music are subject to heavy scrutiny, where anything perceived as offensive to the state's image can result in censorship or even imprisonment. Writers are expected to conform to guidelines that discourage the portrayal of negative aspects of Chinese society, such as corruption, poverty, or the struggles of marginalized groups. Even the depiction of certain historical events, like the Tiananmen Square protests, is forbidden, leaving artists and writers to either self-censor or face the consequences of pushing the boundaries.

For artists, this stifling environment means their creative output must be carefully crafted to avoid offending the government. Many resort to making subtle, indirect critiques through allegory or metaphor. Censorship pressures artists to focus on approved themes like national pride, economic prosperity, or social harmony, leaving little room for exploration of more complex or controversial issues. Writers, too, face similar constraints, often finding it necessary to engage in self-censorship or write in ways that obscure their true intent to avoid detection by the authorities.

In addition to the overt censorship imposed by the state, there is also a societal pressure to conform. Creative works are often subject to review by state-backed entities like the Chinese Writers Association or the Film Bureau, which further curates the acceptable space for creative expression. This creates a stifling environment where the line between artistic integrity and government expectations is constantly blurred.

What Strategies Do Creatives Use to Bypass or Critique Restrictions?

Despite the stifling environment, Chinese artists and writers have developed ingenious strategies to bypass or subtly critique censorship. These methods allow them to continue creating, expressing dissent, or exploring sensitive themes, often in ways that fly under the radar of the authorities.

1. **Allegory and Metaphor**
   One of the most common techniques used by Chinese creatives is the use of allegory and metaphor. By presenting politically sensitive topics in a disguised or symbolic form, writers and artists can avoid direct confrontation with censorship while still conveying their

messages. For instance, novels, films, and artworks may use historical events, fictionalized settings, or abstract concepts to comment on contemporary issues like government corruption, censorship, or human rights abuses. This allows for a level of creativity that still operates within the constraints of the system.

2. **Subtle Critiques through Popular Media**
Many artists and writers use mainstream platforms and popular genres to subtly address sensitive issues. For example, certain popular television shows or movies may incorporate social commentary into their plots, cloaking serious critiques in more universally accepted narratives. A film about a young couple's struggles, for instance, could include subtle references to broader societal issues like the economic divide, urbanization, or environmental concerns without drawing attention from the authorities. By embedding their critiques in light entertainment, creatives can bypass censors while still engaging with the broader public on these important topics.

3. **Digital and Online Platforms**
The rise of digital platforms has created new avenues for creative expression, allowing writers and artists to reach global audiences outside of the traditional censorship channels. Many Chinese creatives have turned to online platforms such as Weibo, WeChat, or even foreign sites like Twitter and Instagram to share their work and connect with others. These platforms, while not entirely free from censorship, offer more flexibility for creators to express themselves and push boundaries compared to state-controlled media. The anonymity and reach of the internet allow for more direct critiques of government policies, social injustices, and controversial topics.

4. **Creating "Underground" Art and Literature**
In the face of direct censorship, some artists and writers

turn to underground movements, where they can explore themes without the threat of state intervention. These underground networks often operate in secrecy, with works being shared in private or limited settings. For instance, authors might circulate banned literature in small circles, or visual artists might display their works in unapproved galleries or through street art. While these works may not gain the mass popularity of state-approved art, they provide a crucial space for free expression and are often seen as symbols of resistance.

5. **International Collaborations and Influence**
Many Chinese artists and writers look to the international community for inspiration and collaboration, using global platforms to bypass local censorship. Some creatives publish their works abroad or collaborate with international artists, allowing their work to reach audiences outside China where censorship is less restrictive. By leveraging these global connections, they can critique issues within China without the immediate fear of government retaliation. These collaborations can also bring attention to Chinese censorship and spark dialogue on a global scale.

6. **Reclaiming Traditional Forms**
Interestingly, some artists and writers in China are turning to traditional Chinese art forms, literature, and philosophy to explore modern issues in ways that are harder for authorities to censor. Ancient Chinese poetry, calligraphy, and classical painting styles, for example, allow for a form of resistance that is grounded in national culture but can subtly critique contemporary social or political problems. By connecting modern challenges to China's long cultural heritage, creatives can bypass censorship in ways that are more acceptable to the state.

The Role of Social Media

In a country where free speech is heavily regulated and dissent is often suppressed, social media platforms in China have become crucial outlets for citizens seeking to express their opinions and organize activism. Despite stringent government controls and censorship, Chinese citizens have found creative ways to use these platforms to challenge official narratives, voice their grievances, and mobilize for social change.

One primary way that Chinese citizens express dissent on social media is by using coded language or indirect messaging. With the Great Firewall of China blocking access to many foreign platforms like Twitter and Facebook, domestic platforms such as WeChat, Weibo, and Douyin (the Chinese version of TikTok) have emerged as the go-to spaces for online discussions. Activists often use euphemisms, puns, or symbolic imagery to bypass automated censorship algorithms. For instance, certain keywords related to controversial topics might be blocked, so users create alternative spellings or employ seemingly unrelated topics to express their messages.

Memes, videos, and viral hashtags have also become powerful tools for organizing and spreading information. The anonymity afforded by the internet allows individuals to share sensitive topics—like labor protests, environmental issues, or human rights abuses—without necessarily exposing their identities. Through viral content, users can highlight underreported stories and push for collective action. However, this activism is often short-lived, as authorities swiftly clamp down on sensitive content, removing posts and even arresting individuals responsible for sharing prohibited material.

Another common tactic is the use of "flash mobs" or grassroots campaigns organized through social media. By rallying supporters online, organizers can quickly mobilize protests, petitions, or other forms of activism. Though many of these events are met with swift police intervention, they still showcase the ability of social media to foster collective action in a society where public gatherings are tightly controlled.

Furthermore, social media also provides a platform for everyday Chinese citizens to hold local officials accountable. Citizens often use platforms like Weibo to post videos or stories documenting corruption, environmental disasters, or other issues that affect their communities. These stories can attract significant public attention, especially when they go viral, putting pressure on authorities to take action.

Some Key Events Where Digital Platforms Have Played a Significant Role?

Over the past decade, several key events in China have demonstrated the power of social media in influencing public opinion, organizing activism, and challenging the status quo.

One of the most notable examples is the **2011 Wenzhou train collision**. In the wake of the tragedy, which killed 40 people and injured nearly 200, the Chinese government's response was widely criticized for its lack of transparency and accountability. As traditional media outlets were censored, citizens turned to Weibo to share images, videos, and stories about the incident. Public outrage grew as people used social media to demand justice and expose the government's attempt to cover up the disaster. The event marked a turning point in Chinese online activism, as it showcased the growing power of social media to bypass state-controlled narratives.

Another significant moment was the **2019 Hong Kong Protests**, although not within mainland China, it had a direct impact on how social media in China was used for activism. Hong Kong citizens, supported by some mainland Chinese youth, used social media platforms to organize protests, raise awareness about the government's encroachment on Hong Kong's autonomy, and communicate with the outside world despite internet restrictions. The protests gained international attention, but Chinese authorities cracked down by censoring related content on social media platforms, especially when it went viral on Weibo. This censorship sparked debates on digital freedom and government control.

The **#MeToo movement in China** also found traction on social media, despite the sensitive nature of the topic. In 2018, when a Chinese woman accused a prominent Peking University professor of sexual assault, the story quickly spread across Weibo, with many other women sharing their experiences of harassment. However, the movement faced severe restrictions as the government moved to censor the discussions, warning users about spreading "rumors." Despite these efforts, the movement continued to resonate, and many women used alternative hashtags to continue the conversation, proving the resilience of online activism.

The **2020 Wuhan COVID-19 outbreak** is another significant event where digital platforms played a crucial role. As the pandemic began in Wuhan, early reports from doctors and whistleblowers circulated on social media, warning about the severity of the outbreak. While authorities initially suppressed these reports, many were shared on platforms like WeChat and Weibo, eventually leading to widespread awareness. The pandemic, which originated in China, led to a digital push for transparency and greater public health communication, though much of the information was still controlled and censored by the government.

Finally, the **Yangtze River Environmental Protests** in 2018-2019 are another example where social media served as a rallying point for activism. When residents of Wuhan discovered that the government planned to build a toxic waste facility near the Yangtze River, they took to social media to organize protests and draw attention to the environmental and health risks. The public outcry was amplified by videos, photos, and coordinated posts on Weibo. Although the protests were quickly suppressed, the digital mobilization raised awareness and added pressure on local authorities to respond.

Gender and LGBTQ+ Issues

Over the past few decades, China has seen some progress in addressing gender and LGBTQ+ issues, though significant challenges remain. The government, social attitudes, and cultural norms all play a role in shaping the discourse around these topics, and the changes that have occurred often reflect a complex balancing act between global influence, traditional values, and state control.

In recent years, gender equality has gained more visibility in public discourse, especially in urban centers. The push for equal opportunities for women in education and the workforce has made strides, with more women attending universities and participating in the job market than ever before. The Chinese government has implemented policies aimed at improving women's rights, such as legislation against domestic violence, which became law in 2016. This marks a significant step in acknowledging and addressing the problem of domestic abuse.

However, traditional gender roles remain deeply ingrained in Chinese society, and gender inequality persists in many areas, particularly in rural regions. Women often face significant pressure to conform to societal expectations of marriage and motherhood, and the "leftover women" stereotype stigmatizes those who remain unmarried past a certain age. Additionally, despite legal advancements, the gender pay gap remains a notable issue, and women in leadership positions are still relatively scarce.

When it comes to LGBTQ+ issues, progress has been slower, and attitudes remain conservative. Homosexuality was decriminalized in 1997, and in 2001, it was removed from the official list of mental illnesses. These legal changes were important milestones, but social acceptance is a different matter. Public opinion toward LGBTQ+ individuals in China can be harsh, with many still viewing homosexuality as a taboo subject, often tied to outdated notions of family honor and societal expectations.

In recent years, the LGBTQ+ community in China has made noticeable strides in visibility and advocacy. Pride events, though largely unofficial, have been held in cities like Shanghai and Beijing, though they are often met with governmental scrutiny or local police interference. Online platforms and social media, especially Weibo and WeChat, have become spaces for LGBTQ+ individuals to connect, share experiences, and advocate for equal rights. However, censorship still limits the extent to which LGBTQ+ issues can be openly discussed, especially when it comes to challenging the state's conservative stance on family values and marriage.

How Do Personal Stories Challenge Societal and Governmental Norms?

Personal stories have a unique power to challenge societal and governmental norms, especially in a country like China where state narratives often dominate public discourse. These stories, whether shared through art, literature, social media, or personal encounters, humanize issues that are otherwise pushed to the periphery of public consciousness. They provide a voice to those who are often marginalized, offering a glimpse into the complexities of gender and LGBTQ+ experiences that are not often portrayed in the media.

For example, the stories of individuals who defy traditional gender roles—such as women who pursue careers over marriage or men who express vulnerability—create a space for conversations about the evolving expectations of gender in China. These personal accounts challenge the societal pressures that push individuals into rigid roles, demonstrating the desire for more freedom of choice and self-expression. Women who speak out about their struggles with the "leftover women" label, or men who share their experiences of breaking free from conventional masculine ideals, not only challenge traditional norms but also raise important questions about how society defines success and identity.

In the case of LGBTQ+ individuals, personal stories are particularly potent in dismantling societal misconceptions. Many Chinese LGBTQ+ individuals who have shared their coming-out stories or experiences of discrimination have made significant contributions to shifting public attitudes. For instance, the rise of openly gay celebrities, although still rare, provides representation that helps normalize diverse sexual orientations. These stories encourage others to consider LGBTQ+ identities not as anomalies but as valid expressions of human experience, fostering empathy and understanding in the wider society.

Moreover, the stories of those who engage in activism or struggle for recognition in the face of governmental censorship further challenge the status quo. Online communities and platforms, despite the government's efforts to control them, allow LGBTQ+ people to connect and build solidarity. Personal blogs, social media posts, and videos that share the lived experiences of LGBTQ+ individuals often transcend the boundaries of state control, allowing for greater exposure to diverse viewpoints. While these platforms are frequently subject to censorship, the very existence of these stories online underscores a growing demand for change in a society that continues to grapple with issues of freedom and expression.

In addition to personal narratives, art and literature also play an important role in challenging norms. Writers, filmmakers, and artists in China who address LGBTQ+ themes or gender inequality often face censorship or backlash but still manage to find creative ways to convey their messages. These stories not only challenge governmental and societal norms but also inspire others to reflect on their own beliefs and experiences, gradually shifting the cultural landscape.

Part IV: The Political Landscape

The Changing Role of Media

State control over media in China has evolved significantly, especially in recent decades, reflecting both the country's rapid modernization and its ongoing commitment to maintaining control over public discourse. Traditionally, Chinese media was tightly controlled, with all major outlets functioning as extensions of government propaganda. The Chinese Communist Party (CCP) has always viewed the media as a tool to uphold its political authority, promote national unity, and maintain social stability. However, the role and reach of state control have adapted to the changing technological landscape and the increasingly interconnected global environment.

In the past, the government's control over media was straightforward and direct. Print journalism, television, and radio broadcasts were predominantly state-run, and outlets were required to adhere strictly to the party's ideology and priorities. While the media's primary function was to propagate government-approved messages, any content considered subversive or critical of the party was swiftly censored.

In recent years, the rise of digital media has brought new challenges and opportunities for both the government and the public. With the advent of the internet and social media platforms, Chinese citizens gained access to a wealth of information beyond state-run outlets. This shift prompted the government to tighten its grip on online content more rigorously. Today, the "Great Firewall" blocks foreign websites and social media platforms like Facebook, Twitter, and Google, while domestic platforms such as Weibo, WeChat, and Baidu are closely monitored and censored. The government employs an army of internet censors to remove content that contradicts the state's narrative or raises questions about sensitive topics such as political dissent, corruption, or human rights violations.

In addition to censorship, the government has also taken a more proactive role in shaping public discourse. The use of algorithms, the introduction of surveillance technologies, and the increasing pressure on journalists and bloggers have all contributed to a media environment where self-censorship is commonplace. In recent years, investigative journalism has been stifled, with many reporters facing harassment or imprisonment for attempting to expose corruption or other sensitive issues.

The evolution of state control over media has also been influenced by global trends, such as the rise of digital media and citizen journalism. The government has responded by developing its own narrative control mechanisms, including the promotion of pro-government influencers and the deployment of paid commentators to sway public opinion. While these tactics have allowed the CCP to maintain a high degree of control over public perception, they have also faced criticism for stifling genuine debate and limiting access to objective news sources.

Examples of Investigative Journalism That Reveal Hidden Truths?

Despite the heavy restrictions on journalism in China, there have been instances where brave journalists and whistleblowers have managed to reveal hidden truths that challenge the official narrative. While these examples are relatively rare, they underscore the determination of individuals to expose corruption, human rights abuses, and environmental disasters that the government seeks to conceal.

One notable example is the coverage of environmental pollution and its devastating impact on public health. In 2015, the investigative journalist Liu Renwen exposed the illegal dumping of toxic waste in several rural areas in China, resulting in severe contamination of the water supply. Liu's work was widely shared on social media, and although some of the material was censored, the public's reaction to the revelations brought more attention to environmental issues. The investigation led to some local government officials being dismissed, though the broader systemic problems related to pollution and environmental governance remained largely unaddressed.

Another example comes from the coverage of labor conditions in China's factories. Journalists like Li Xueqing have worked undercover in sweatshops and reported on labor exploitation, including poor working conditions, underpayment, and even forced labor in some industries. Li's reports, published on independent blogs and foreign news outlets, shed light on the dark side of China's manufacturing boom, revealing the human toll behind the country's economic miracle. Despite the risks involved in such investigations, these pieces of journalism have brought international attention to issues that the Chinese government prefers to keep hidden.

The case of corruption within the Chinese political elite is also an area where investigative journalism has made an impact. In 2012, a Chinese journalist named Zhao Lianhai exposed the scandal of tainted milk powder, which caused widespread harm to children. Zhao's investigation brought to light not only the negligent practices of the dairy industry but also the failure of regulatory bodies to enforce safety standards. His work was instrumental in forcing the government to take action, leading to the prosecution of several corporate executives and the implementation of stricter regulations. However, Zhao was later imprisoned for his efforts, highlighting the risks involved in exposing sensitive issues.

More recently, the crackdown on the #MeToo movement in China has prompted investigative journalists to uncover instances of sexual harassment and abuse in universities and workplaces. In 2018, independent outlets began to report on the allegations of harassment by prominent figures in the entertainment and academic industries. While many of these reports were censored within China, they gained significant traction abroad, revealing how gender inequality and abuse of power persist despite the government's attempts to suppress the conversation.

These examples of investigative journalism reveal the vital role of the press in holding powerful entities accountable, even in the face of intense state control. They illustrate how determined journalists and activists continue to fight for transparency and justice, often at great personal risk. Although the challenges are immense, the persistence of these journalists in exposing hidden truths shows the importance of independent journalism in a society where information is carefully curated and controlled by the state.

China's Foreign Policy and Hidden Agendas

China's foreign policy plays a crucial role in shaping its domestic narratives, reinforcing national identity, government legitimacy, and public perceptions of global affairs. The Chinese Communist Party (CCP) strategically aligns its international stance with domestic messaging, using state-controlled media, education, and censorship to shape public opinion.

How China's Foreign Policy Influences Domestic Narratives

1. **Nationalism and Party Legitimacy**
   China often portrays its foreign policy as a struggle against Western hegemony, reinforcing national pride and justifying the CCP's leadership. State media emphasizes China's rise as a global power while portraying Western nations, particularly the U.S., as adversarial forces seeking to contain China. This narrative strengthens domestic support for the government and fosters a sense of unity.
2. **The "Century of Humiliation" and Historical Justifications**
   The government frequently references historical grievances, such as the Opium Wars and foreign occupation, to frame modern foreign policy decisions.

This historical context is used to validate assertive actions in regions like Taiwan, the South China Sea, and Hong Kong, positioning China as reclaiming its rightful place on the world stage.

3. **Economic Development and Global Influence**
Foreign policy initiatives like the Belt and Road Initiative (BRI) are framed domestically as evidence of China's growing influence and economic strength. Media narratives emphasize how these policies benefit China's economy while also aiding developing nations, reinforcing the idea that China is a responsible global leader.

4. **Control of Information and Perception Management**
The CCP tightly controls information on foreign affairs, filtering negative international coverage while promoting state-approved narratives. For example, China's stance on Taiwan is heavily censored within the country, with alternative views suppressed. Similarly, international criticism of China's human rights policies in Xinjiang is countered with state-driven narratives portraying the region's policies as necessary for stability.

5. **Crisis Management and Narrative Shaping**
When facing diplomatic crises—such as trade disputes with the U.S. or tensions with neighboring countries—China crafts narratives of resilience and self-sufficiency. The government often frames economic or political challenges as attempts by external forces to weaken China, urging the public to rally around the party and embrace domestic alternatives.

Perspectives from Insiders and International Observers

1. **Domestic Scholars and Officials**
   Chinese academics and government officials generally align with the official stance, emphasizing

China's peaceful rise and the importance of national sovereignty. Some, however, advocate for a more pragmatic approach to diplomacy, cautioning against overly aggressive posturing that could harm China's economic interests.

2. **State Media and Public Sentiment**
Outlets like *Xinhua* and *People's Daily* reinforce state narratives, while platforms like WeChat and Weibo provide a space for controlled public discourse. While there is some room for debate, censorship ensures that dissenting views remain marginal. Nationalist sentiment, often encouraged by the state, can lead to public support for hardline policies, such as military exercises near Taiwan or economic retaliation against Western sanctions.

3. **International Scholars and Policy Experts**
Western analysts often highlight how China's foreign policy narratives serve internal political goals, reinforcing the CCP's legitimacy and suppressing dissent. Some scholars argue that China's focus on historical grievances and nationalism could backfire, leading to rigid policies that limit diplomatic flexibility. Others point out that China's control of information makes it difficult for its citizens to critically engage with global issues, leading to a population that views the world through a state-approved lens.

4. **Foreign Governments and Media**
Many international governments view China's foreign policy narratives as a strategic effort to expand influence while maintaining strict domestic control. Reports from organizations like Human Rights Watch and the UN have criticized China's suppression of information, particularly concerning human rights.

Meanwhile, global media outlets often contrast China's official stance with leaked reports and independent investigations, providing alternative perspectives.

The Future of Free Speech in China

Chinese citizens are finding new ways to engage with sensitive topics, often using coded language, satire, or digital platforms outside government control. While censorship remains strict, the emergence of alternative narratives suggests a shift in how people navigate restrictions. Social media, despite heavy monitoring, provides fleeting moments of discussion before posts are deleted, highlighting both the resilience and limitations of public discourse.

The future of free speech in China presents both obstacles and possibilities. Technological advancements give authorities greater control over information, but they also create cracks in the system where ideas can spread. Economic and social pressures may push for more openness in specific areas, such as business and academia, though direct political dissent remains risky. The balance between state control and public expression continues to evolve, shaped by both government policies and the ingenuity of those seeking to communicate beyond imposed boundaries.

Conclusion

A Call to Awareness and Empathy

Supporting free speech and amplifying silenced voices requires active engagement in conversations that challenge censorship and suppression. Readers can cultivate awareness by seeking out diverse perspectives, particularly those that are marginalized or restricted. Engaging with independent journalism, sharing underrepresented stories, and advocating for transparent policies help create an environment where free expression thrives. Challenging misinformation and fostering respectful dialogue also strengthens the foundation of open discourse.

Understanding China's hidden narratives provides a lens into the complexities of restricted information and controlled narratives. Exploring the stories of individuals who resist suppression fosters a deeper appreciation for struggles against censorship worldwide. This awareness encourages a more nuanced global perspective, where empathy extends beyond borders and cultural differences. By recognizing the universal desire for truth and freedom, individuals can become allies in the pursuit of a more open and informed world.

Made in the USA
Monee, IL
16 March 2025

14099896R00036